THOMAS JEFFERSON

by Candice Ransom

Cody Koala

An Imprint of Pop!

popbooksonline.com

abdopublishing.com

Published by Pop!, a division of ABDO, PO Box 398166, Minneapolis, Minnesota 55439. Copyright © 2019 by POP, LLC. International copyrights reserved in all countries. No part of this book may be reproduced in any form without written permission from the publisher. Pop!™ is a trademark and logo of POP, LLC.

Printed in the United States of America, North Mankato, Minnesota

042018
092018

THIS BOOK CONTAINS
RECYCLED MATERIALS

Cover Photo: GraphicaArtis/Getty Images
Interior Photos: GraphicaArtis/Getty Images, 1; iStockphoto, 5; Shutterstock Images, 6, 11, 15, 19 (top), 19 (bottom left), 19 (bottom right), 21 (top), 21 (bottom left); North Wind Picture Archives, 9, 12, 16, 21 (bottom right).

Editor: Charly Haley
Series Designer: Laura Mitchell

Library of Congress Control Number: 2017963382

Publisher's Cataloging-in-Publication Data

Names: Ransom, Candice, author.
Title: Thomas Jefferson / by Candice Ransom.
Description: Minneapolis, Minnesota : Pop!, 2019. | Series: Founding fathers | Includes online resources and index.
Identifiers: ISBN 9781532160202 (lib.bdg.) | ISBN 9781532161322 (ebook) |
Subjects: LCSH: Jefferson, Thomas, 1743-1826--Juvenile literature. | Founding Fathers of the United States--Juvenile literature. | Statesmen--United States--Biography--Juvenile literature. | United States--Politics and government--1783-1789--Juvenile literature.
Classification: DDC 973.4 [B]--dc23

Cody Koala

Pop open this book and you'll find QR codes like this one, loaded with information, so you can learn even more!

Scan this code* and others like it while you read, or visit the website below to make this book pop.

popbooksonline.com/thomas-jefferson

*Scanning QR codes requires a web-enabled smart device with a QR code reader app and a camera.

Table of Contents

Growing Up

As a child, Thomas Jefferson liked to walk and ride horses.

Watch a video here!

Thomas designed this home called Monticello.

Thomas grew up in Virginia. Virginia was a **colony** in America. Great Britain ruled the American colonies.

War

Americans thought the British king made unfair laws. They went to war with the British. It was called the **American Revolutionary War**.

Learn more here!

Jefferson wrote the **Declaration of Independence**. It said that America was its own country, separate from Great Britain. Jefferson worked many days to write it.

America won the war. The new country was called the United States of America.

Chapter 3

A Bigger Country

Jefferson became the first US **Secretary of State**. He worked on America's relationships with other countries.

Later, Jefferson became America's second vice president.

Complete an activity here!

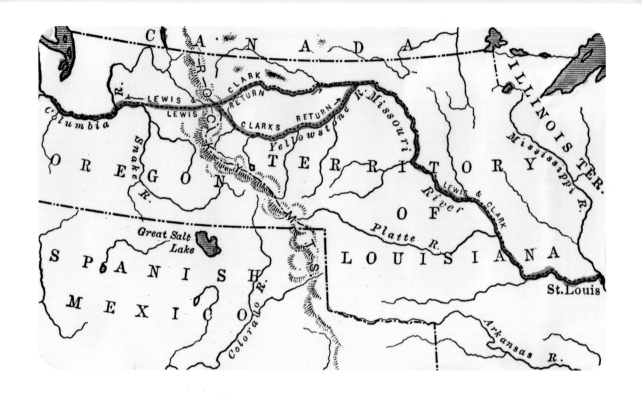

Jefferson became the third president of the United States in 1801. The United States needed room to grow.

Jefferson bought more land to the west. It made the country twice as big. Americans did not know much about the West. Jefferson sent men to explore the **territory**.

Chapter 4

America Today

Jefferson died on July 4, 1826. This was exactly 50 years after the United States declared independence.

Learn more here!

Jefferson was a **Founding Father**. He worked hard to shape our country. Jefferson helped the United States grow into the country that it is today.

Jefferson was also an inventor. He created a clock, farming tools, furniture, and other things.

On April 13,
Jefferson
was born in
Virginia.

Jefferson became
president of the
United States.

On July 4,
Jefferson died
at his home.

1743

1801

1826

1776

1803

Jefferson wrote the
Declaration of Independence.

Jefferson bought
western lands.

Making Connections

Text-to-Self

This book talks about Jefferson's life as a child. How is your life like Jefferson's? How is it different?

Text-to-Text

Have you read other books about people from the past? What can you learn from those books?

Text-to-World

Jefferson was a Founding Father. What did he do to change the world you live in?

Glossary

American Revolutionary War – the war fought between the colonies and Great Britain.

colony – land ruled by another country.

Declaration of Independence – a document that said America is its own country.

Founding Father – one of the people who helped create the US government.

Secretary of State – a person in the US government who guides America's relationships with other countries.

territory – an area that belongs to a country.

Index

Online Resources

popbooksonline.com

Thanks for reading this Cody Koala book!

Scan this code* and others like it in this book, or visit the website below to make this book pop!

popbooksonline.com/thomas-jefferson

*Scanning QR codes requires a web-enabled smart device with a QR code reader app and a camera.